NUMBER 716

THE ENGLISH EXPERIENCE

ITS RECORD IN EARLY PRINTED BOOKS
PUBLISHED IN FACSIMILE

JOHN BRADFORD

A SERMON
OF REPENTANCE

(n.p.), (1553)

WALTER J. JOHNSON, INC.

THEATRUM ORBIS TERRARUM, LTD.

AMSTERDAM 1975 NORWOOD, N.J.

The publishers acknowledge their gratitude to
the Curators of the Bodleian Library, Oxford,
for their permission to reproduce the Library's
copy, Shelfmark: 8°.Z.197 Art BS (5)

S.T.C. No. 3496

Collation: A⁴,B-H⁸

Published in 1975 by

Theatrum Orbis Terrarum, Ltd.
Keizersgracht 526, Amsterdam

&

Walter J. Johnson, Inc.
355 Chestnut Street
Norwood, New Jersey
07648

Printed in the Netherlands

ISBN: 90 221 0716 7

Library of Congress Catalog Card Number
74-28835

¶ A Sermon

of repentaunce, made by
John Bradforde.

(*)

Luke. xiii.

Except you repent you shall all
lykewyse perysshe.

Apoc. ii.

Remembre whence thou arte fallen, and repente thee.

¶ To the Christian reader, John Bradford wyscheth the true knowledge and peace of Iesus Christ, oure alone and omni sufficiente sauiour.

Greate and heauy is Goddes anger agaynste vs, as the most greuous plague of ÿ death of our late kynge (a Prince of all that euer was sithen christes ascention into heauen in anye region pereles) nowe fallen vpon vs, doth pronosticate. For when Goddes iudgemente hath begonne wyth hys chylde thus oure deare dea   yng, lette othermen thynke as they c   , I surely cannot be perswaded otherwyse, but that a greuous & bitter cuppe of Gods vengeaunce is ready to be powred out for vs Englishmen to drynke of. The whelpe God hath beaton to fraye the bandogge. Iudgemente is begonne at Gods house. In goddes mercy to hym wardes he is take away, that his eyes shuld not see, the miseries we shall fele: he was to good to tarrye with vs so wycked, so frowarde, so peruerse, so ob stinate,

.Pe.iiii.

.rt.

ffinate, so malicious, so hypocriticall,
so couetous, vncleane, vntrue, prowde
carnall.&c.a generatiõ. I wyll not goe
aboute to paynte vs oute in oure cou-
lours. All the worlde which neuer saw
England, by heare saye seeth Englãd.
God by his plagues and vengeaunce I
feare me wyll paynte vs oute, & poynte
vs oute, we haue so mocked with hym
and his Gospell, that we shal feele it is
no bourdyng with him, Of longe tyme
we haue couered our couetousnes and
carnalitie, vnder ÿ cloke of his gospell,
so that al men shal see vs to our shame,
when he shall take his gospell awaye,
and geue it to a people that wyll bring
forth the frutes of it, then shall we ap-
peare as we be. To let his gospell tary
with vs, he can not, for we despyse it,
contempne it, are glutted with it, we
disdayne his Manna, it is but a vyle
meate thynke we: we would be agayne
in Egipte, and syt by the greasy flesshe
pottes, to eate agayn our garlike, oni-
ons, and leekes. Sithen gods gospell
came amongest vs, we saye nowe we
had neuer plenty, therefore agayne let
vs goe and worshyp the quene of hea-
uen. Childrẽ beginne to gather stickes Ie. xliiii.
the fathers kyndle the fyer, & the we- Hie. vii.
men make ÿ cakes to offer to the quene

of heauen, and to prouoke the lozde to
anger. The earthe can not abyde nowe
the wozdes and sermons of Amos: the
cause of all rebellion is Amos and
his preaching. It is Paule and his fe-
lowes, that makes all oute of ozder.
Summa, the gospell is nowe παντ$ρ
πε$ι$ψημα and κ$θ$θ$ρ$μα τοῦ κο$τ$μ$εν the
outcaste and curse of the realme: and
so are the preachers, therfoze out of the
doozes with them. So that I saye, god
can not let his gospel tary with vs, but
must nedes take it awaye to do vs some
pleasure therein, foz so shall we thinke
foz a time: as ẏ Sodomitanes thought
when Lot departed frō them, as the old
wozld thought whē Noe crept into his
arcke: as ẏ Ierosolomptanes thought
whē ẏ apostles wente thence to Pella.
Then were thei mery, then was al pa-
stime: When Moyses was absent, then
wēt they to eating & dzinking, & rose a-
gayne to playe. Then was all peace, all
was well, nothynge amysse. But alas,
sodenlye came the sloude and dzowned
them, Gods wzath waxed hote againste
them. Then was weale awaye, mour-
nynge and woe: then was cryeng out,
wzinging of hādes, renting of clothes,
sobbing and sighynge foz the miseries
fallen, out of the whiche they could not
scape

Am.vii.

Act.xvii.

Gen.xix.
gen.vi.

Ex.xxxii.

scape. But oh you mourners and criers
out: ye renters of clothes, why mourne
you? what is the cause of your misery?
The gospell is gone, goddes woorde is
lytle preached, you were not disquieted
with it? Noe troubleth you not, Lot is
departed, the apostles are gone: what
nowe is the cause of these your miseries? Wyll you at the length confesse it
is your sinnes? Nape now it is to late.
God called vpon you and you woulde
not heare hym, therefore yell and crye
out now, for he wil not heare you: You
bowed your eares frō hearyng of gods
law, therfore your prayer is execrable.
But to come again to vs Englishmen,
I feare me I say, for oure vnthankful-
nes sake, for our impietie and wickednes, as god hath take away our kinge,
so will he take awaye his gospel: yea so
we would haue it, thē shoulo al be well
thinke manye. Well, if he take that a-
waye, for a tyme perchaunce we shall
be quiet, but at length we shall fele the
want to our woe, at lēgth he wyll haue
at vs, as at Sodome, at Ierusalem, and
other places And now he beginneth to
brew such a brewing, wherin one ofvs
is like to destroy an other, and so make
an open gappe for forren enemies to
deuoure vs, and destroy vs. The father
is

is agaynste the sonne , the brother a-
gaynste the brother. And Lorde wyth
what conscience? Oh be thou mercifull vnto vs , and in thyne anger remember thy mercye, suffre thy selfe to
be intreated, be reconciled vnto vs, nay
reconcile vs vnto the. Oh thou god of
iustice, iudge iustlye, oh thou sonne of
god which camest to destroye the wor-
i. Joh. iii kes of Sathan, destroye his furoures
nowe smokynge, and almoste sette on
fyre in this realme. We haue synned,
we haue sinned, and therfore arte thou
angrye. Oh be not angry for euer. Geue vs peace, peace, peace, in the lord, set
vs to warre agaynste synne, agaynste
Sathan, againste our carnall despres,
and geue vs the victory this way. This
victory we obtayn by faith. This faith
is not without repentaunce, as hir gē-
telman vssher before hyr. Before hyr.
I say in discerning true fayth frō false
fayth, lyppe fayth, Englishmens faith:
for els it spzynges oute of true fayth.
This vssher then of repentaunce, if we
trulye possessed, we should be certayne
of true fayth, and so assured of the vic-
torye ouer death, hell, and Sathan: his
workes then which he hath styred vp,
wonld quayle: God woulde restore vs
politike peace, right should be right ꝺ
haue

haue right, gods gospel should tarry w̄
vs, religion shuld be cherished, super-
stition suppressed, and so we yet sothing
happye, not withstandinge the greate
losse of our moste graciouse liege soue-
raygne Lorde. All these woulde come
to passe you se, yf the gentleman v sther
I speake of, I meane repētaūce, where
at ynne with vs. As if he be absēt, we
may be certain that lady sath is absent
wherfore we cā not but be vanquished
of the world, the flesh, and the deuyll,
and so will Sathans workes prosper
though not in al thinges, to bleare our
eyes, yet in that thinge which, he most
of all despreth. Therfore to repentaūce
for our selues priuatelye, and for the
realme and church publikelye, euery
one shoulde laboure to styrre vp both
our selues & others. This, to the ende
that for my parte I might help, I haue
presently put forth a sermon of repentaunce, whiche hath lyen by me halfe a
yeare at the leaste, for the most part of
it. For the laste sommer as I was a-
broade preaching in the countreye, my
chaunce was to make a sermon of repentaunce the whiche was ernestlye
of diuers despred of me, that I shoulde
geue it them written or els put it forth
in print. The whiche thing to graunt,

a a

as I could not (for I had not wrytté it)
so I told thē that had so ernestli desired
it. But whē no naye woulde serue, but
I muste promise them to wryte it as I
could: I consented to theyr request that
they should haue it at my leasure. This
leasure I prolonged so longe, that as I
wene I offended thē, so did I please my
selfe, as one more gladde to reade other
mēnes wrytinges, then in such sorte to
publysh my wrytinges for other men to
reade, not that I woulde others not to
profyt by me: but that I knowing how
shorte my suppeller & store is, would be
loth for the enemies to haue iuste occasion of euyll speakinge & wresting that
whiche simple is spoken. But when I
considered this present time, to occasiō
men now to loke vpō all things in such
sorte as might moue them to godlines,
rather then to anye curiouse questio-
ning, I for ÿ satisfyeng of my promise,
& profytinge of the simple ignoraunt &
rude, haue nowe caused this Sermō to
be prynted, the which I beseche god for
his Christes sake , to vse as a meane
wherby of his mercy it may please him
to worke in me & many others true hartye repētaūce for our sinnes, to the glory of his name. Thus fare thou wel
in the Lord. The .rii. of Julie.
Anno. M.D.LIII.

❧ A sermon of repentaũce made by John Bradforde.

THe lyfe we haue at this present, is the gyft of God, in whom we liue moue, and are, Actes. xvii. and therfore is he called Iehouah, Exod iii. for the whiche lyfe, as we shoulde be thankefull, so we may not in any wyse, vse it after our one fantaci, but to theende for the whiche it is geuen & lente vs, that is, to the settynge forthe of gods prayse and glory, by repentaunce, conuersion, and obedience to his good wyl, and holy lawes, where vnto his longe sufferynge doeth (as it were) euen drawe vs, yf our hartes by impenitency were not hardned. And therfore our lyfe in the scripture

is called a walkynge, for that as
the bodye dayly draweth more &
more neare hys ende, that is the
earth: euen so oure soule draweth
daylye more and more, neare the
death, that is: saluation or damp
nation heauen or hell. Of whiche
thinge, in that we are moost care
lesse, and very foles (for we alas,
are the same to daye, we were yesterdaye, and not better or nearer
to God, but rather nearer to hell,
Sathan, and perdition, beynge
couetouse, idle, carnall, secure, ne-
cligēt, proud, &c.) I thinke my la
bour cannot be better bestowed,
then with the Baptist, Christ Ie
sus, and his Apostels, to harp on
this stringe, whyche of all other
is mooste necessarye, and that in
these dayes moste specially. What
strynge is that sayeth one ? Forsoth brother the Strynge of repen-
tannce

taunce, ý whiche Christ our sauiour did vse first in hys ministery, and as his minister at this present I wyll vse vnto you all.

Repent, for the kingdome of heauen is at hande. Math. iiii.

This sentence thus pronounced, and preached by our sauiour Jesus Chryste, as it doeth commaund vs to repent, so to the doinge of the same, it sheweth vs a sufficient cause to sturre vs vppe therevnto namelye, for that the kyngdome of heauen (which is a kyngedome of all ioye, peace, ryches, power, and pleasure) is at hande, to al such as do so, that is, as do repente. So that the meanynge hereof is, as thoughe oure sauiour myght thus speake presently: Syrs, for that I se you all walkynge the wronge way, euen to Sathan and vnto hell fyre, by

B.ii.   folo=

folowynge the kyngedome of
Sathan, whiche nowe is colou-
red vnder the pylled pleasures
of this lyfe, and folyshnes of the
flesshe, moste subtelly to your vtter vndoynge, and destruction:
Beholde and marke well what
I saye vnto you: The kingdome
of heauen that is a nother maner
of ioye and felicitie, honoure, and
riches, power, and, pleasure, then
you nowe perceyue or enioye, is
euen at hande, and at youre bac-
kes, as yf you wyll turne agayn,
that is, repent you, you shal most
trulye and pleasauntlye fele, see,
and enherit: Turne agayne there
fore I say, that is: repent, for this
ioye I speake of, euen the kyngdome of heauen, is at hande.

　　Here we maye note fyrste the
corruption of our nature, in that
to this commaundement, repent
　　　　　　　　　　you,

you, he addeth a cause, for ý kingdome of heauen is at hande: for
by reason of the corruption and
sturdines of our nature, God vnto all his commaundementes cō-
monlye epther addeth some promise to prouoke vs to abedience,
or elles some such sufficient cause
as cannot but tickle vs vp to
hartye labourynge, for the doing
of the same: as here to the commaundement of doynge penaūce
he addeth this aitiologie or cause
sayinge: for the kyngdome of
heauen is at hande.

Agayne in that he ioyneth to the
commaundemente, the cause,
saynge: for the kyngedome of
heauē is at hand: we maye learne
that of the kyngdome of heauen
none (to whome the ministerye of
preaching doth apperetayne) can
be partaker, but such as repente

    B.iii.   and

and do pennaunce.

Therefore dearlye beloued, yf you regarde the kyngedome of heauen, in that you cannot entre there in excepte you repent, I befech you al of euery estate as you woulde your owne weale, to repent and do penaunce, the whych thinge that you maye do, I wyll do my beste nowe to helpe you by gods grace.

But fyrste because we cannot well tell what repentaunce is, thorowe ignoraunce, & for lacke of knoweledge, and false teachynge, I wyll (to begynne with all, shewe you what repentaunce is.

Repentaunce or pennaunce is no Englyshe worde, but we borowe it of the Latinistes, to whome pennaunce is afore thinkynge in Englyshe, in Greke, a
be=

beynge wyſe afterwardes, in He-
brewe: a conuerſion or turnynge,
the whyche conuerſion or turnynge, in that it can not be true
and hartye vnto God eſpeciallye,
without ſome good hope or truſt
of pardone for that whyche is
all readye doone and paſte, I
maye well in thys ſorte deſyne
it, namelye, that pennaunce is a
ſorrowynge or forethynkynge
of oure ſynnes paſte, an earneſte
purpoſe to amende, or turnynge
to G O D, with a truſte of pardone.

    This diffinicion maye be
deuyded into thre partes, that
pennaunce or repentaunce ſhuld
contayne, fyrſte a ſorowynge for
our ſynnes: Secondlye a truſte
of pardonne, whyche otherwyſe
maye be called a perſwaſyon

of Gods mercy, by the merits of
Christe, for the forgeuenesse of
our synnes: And thyrdely apur-
pose to amende, or conuersion to
a newe lyfe: the whiche thyrde or
last parte, cannot be called proper
ly a parte, for it is but an effect of
pennaunce, as towardes the ende
you shall se by Gods grace. But
least suche as seke for occasion to
speake euill, shoulde haue any occasion, though thei tarry not out
the ende of this sermon: I there
fore deuyde penaunce into the
iii, foresayde partes, of sorowing
for our synne, of good hoope or
truste of pardon, and of a newe
lyfe. Thus you now se what penaunce is, a sorowyng for synne,
a purpose to amend, with a good
hoope or truste of pardone.

This pennaunce not onely dif
fereth from that whiche men co-
monlye

onlye haue taken to be penaunce, in saying and doing our
nioyned lady psalters , Seuen
Psalmes, fastinges, pilgrimages
those dedes and suche lyke thin
ges: but also frome that whiche
the moze learned haue declared
to consist of thzee partes, namely
Contricion, Confession and Satisfaction.

Contricion they call a iuste &
a full sozowe foz theyz synne, foz
this wozde, iust, and ful, is one of
the differences betwene contrition and attricion.

Confession they cal a numbzing
of all theyz synnes in the eare of
theyz gohstly fhther: foz as (saye
they) a iudge cánot absolue with
out knoweledge of the cause oz
matter, so cannot the Pzeiste oz
goslly father absolue from other
synnes , then those whiche hee

B.b.   Doth

doth heare.

Satisfaction they call a mennes makinge vnto God for theyr synnes, by theyr vndue workes *opera indebita*, workes more thē they nede to doe, as they term them. This is theyr pennaunce whyche they preache, wryte, and alowe: but howe true this grace is, howe it agreeth wyth goddes woorde, howe it is to be alowed, taughte, preached, and wrytten, let vs a lyttell consydre. If a man repent not vntyll he haue a iust & full sorowynge for his synnes (dearly beloued) when shall he repent: for inasmuche as hell fier, and the ponyshment of the deuils is a iuste ponyshmente for synne: Inasmuch as in al synne, ther is a contempte of G O D, whyche is all goodnesse: and therefore there is a deserte of all ylnesse:

Alasse

Alasse who can bear oʒ feele this iuste soʒowe, this full soʒowe foʒ our sinnes, this their contrition, whyche they so do discerne from theyʒ attriction ⁊ Shall not man by this doctrine rather dispayʒe then come by repentaunce⁊

Yf a manne repente not vntyll he haue made confessyon of all hys synnes, in the eare of hys goost-lye father: yf a man can not haue absolution of hys synnes, vntyll hys synnes be tolde by tale and nūber, in the pꝛestes eare, in that as Dauyd sayethe, none canne vnderstande, moche lesse then btter all hys synnes. Delicta quis intelligit. Who can vnderstande his synnes⁊in that Dauid of him selfe complayneth (else where,) howe that thys synnes are ouer flowed hys head, and as a heauye

Psa. rir.
Psalm.
rrbiii.

but⁊

burthen do depzesse hym: halasse
shall not a man by this doctryne
be vtterlye dzyuen from repentaunce ? Thoughe they haue
gone aboute somethyng to make
plaisters foz theyz soozes, of confession, oz attricion, to aswage
this gere, biddinge a manne to
hope well of his contricion, thou
ghe it be not so ful, as is requered
and of his confession, thoughe he
haue not nombzed all his sinnes,
yf so be that he do so muche as in
hym lyeth: Dearelye beloued in
that there is none but that herein he is gyltye (foz who doth as
muche as he maye) trowe ye that
this playster is not lyke salte foz
soze eyes ? Yes vndoubtedlye
when they haue al done they can
foz the appeasing of consciences
in these pointes, this is the some
that we yet shoulde hope well.

But

But yet so hope that we muste
stonde in a mammerynge & doubtynge, whether oure synnes be
forgeuen. For to beleue, remissio-
nem peccatorum, that is to be cer-
teyne of forgeuenes of sinnes, as
oure crede teacheth vs, they cout
it a presumptió. Oh abhominati-
on, and that not only hereat, but
at al theyr pennaúce as they paynte it.

    As concerninge Satisfaction
by theyr opera indebita, vndewe
workes, that is by suche workes
as they nede not to doo, but of
theyr owne voluntarynesse, and
wylfulnesse (wylfulnesse in dede)
who seeth not monsteuous abho
mination, blasphemie, and euen
epen fyghtynge agaynste God.
For yf Satisfaction can be done
by man, then Christ died in vaine
for hym that so satisfieth, and so
        saigneth

reygneth he in vayne, is he a byſ-
ſhoppe and a Prieſte in vayne.

Deu. vi.
Mat. xxii.
Mar. xx.
Luke. x. Goddes lawe requyreth loue to
God wyth all oure harte, ſoule,
power, myghte, and ſtrenghte, ſo
that there is nothynge canne be
done to Godwarde, whyche is
not conteyned in this commaundemente, nothinge can be done o-
uer, and aboue this.

Agayne Chriſt requireth that
Joh. xiii to manward we ſhoulde loue one
another, as he loued vs. Trowe
that we can do anye good thynge
to our neyghbourwarde, whyche
is not herein compriſed:

Yea, lette them tell me when
they do any thynge ſo in the loue
of God and theyr neyghboure,
but that they had nede to crye,
Mat. vi. Dimitte nobis debita noſtra.

Forgeue vs oure ſinnes, ſo farre
are we of, from ſatiſſieng, doeth
not

not Chryste saye, when you haue done all thinges that I haue commaunded you, saye that ye be but vnprofitable seruauntes. Put no thinge to my worde, sayeth God. Yes, workes of supererogation, superabhomination saye they. Whatsoeuer thinges are true sayeth the apostle saynct Paul. Philip. iiii. whatsoeuer thynges are honeste, whatsoeuer thynges are pure, whatsoeuer thynges are conueniente, whatsoeuer thinges are of honeste report, yf there be anye bertue, yf there bee anye prayse, haue you them in youre minde and do them, and the God of peace shalbe with you. I ween this well looked on, wyll pull vs from popishe satisfactory workes whyche do deface Chrystes treasures and satisfaction.

In

Lu. xvii.

Ap. xxii.
Deu. iiii.
xii.

In heauen and in earth was there none founde that coulde satiſfy gods anger for our ſinnes or get heauen for man, but only ẙ ſonne of God Jeſus Chriſt, the Lyon of the tribe of Juda, who by his bloude hath wrought the worke of satiſfaction, and alone-lye is worthy all honour, glorye, and prayſe, for he hath opened the boke with the ſeuen ſeales, Apoca.v.

Dearely beloued, therfore ab-hore this abhominacion, euē to thincke that there is any other ſa tiſfaction to Godwarde for ſinne then Chriſtes bloude only: blaſ-phemye it is, and that horriblye to thynke otherwyſe.

The bloud of Chriſt purifieth (ſayeth S. John) from al ſinne, and therfore he is called ẙ lambe Apo. xiii ſlayne from the begynnynge of the

the worlde , becauſe there was neuer ſynne forgeuen of God , nor
ſhalbe from the begynnynge vnto the ende of the worlde , but only thorowe Chriſtes death, prate
the pope ʒ hys prelates as pleaſe
them , with theyr pardons , pur-
gatories,purgations,placebots,
irentales, diriges, workes of ſu-
pererogations , ſuperabhomina-
tions.ʒc.

Cʒap.rliii. I am he ſayeth the
Lorde , whiche put awaye thyne
offences, and that for myne owne
ſake , and wyll no more remembre thyne iniquities ꞉ putte me
in remembraunce (for we wyll
reaſon together) and tel me what
thou haſte for thee , to make thee
ryghtuous. Thy fyrſte father offended ſore.ʒc. And thus wryteth
Saynt John, yf any man ſynne ſ.Joḧ.ii.
we haue an aduocate ſayth he
           C   with

with the father, euen Jesus chrst
the ryghtuous, and he is the propiciation or satisfaction for oure
synnes: As in the. iiii. chapter, he
sayeth, that God hath sente hys
Sonne to be a propiciation or
meane, for the takynge awaye of
oure synnes, accordynge to that
whyche Paule wryteth. Hebr. ii.
where he calleth Chryst, a mercifull and faythfull priest, to purge
the peoples synnes, so that blinde
bussardes, and peruerse papistes
they bee, whyche yet wyll prate
our merites or workes to satisfy
for our sinnes in part or in whole
before baptisme or after. For to o-
myt the testimonies I broughte
out of John and Paule, whyche
the blinde cannot but see: I pray
you remember the texte oute of
Esaye, whyche euen nowe I re-
hearsed, beynge spoken to suche
as

as were the the people of God, ꝙ
had ben a long time, but yet were
fallen into greuous synnes after
theyr adoption into the number
of gods chyldrē, it is for my own
sake sayth God, that I put away
thy sinnes. Wher is your parting
of the stake nowꞓif it be for gods
owne sake, yf Christe be the pro=
pitiation, then recant, except you
wyll become ydolaters, makinge
your workes God, and Chryste=
Saye as Dauid teacheth: not
to vs lorde, nat to vs, but to thy
name be the glorye.

And it is to be noted that God
dothe caste in their teeth, euen
the synne of theyr fyrste father,
leaste they shoulde thynke that
yet perchaunce, for the ryght=
uousnes and goodnes of theyr
good fathers, theyr synnes
wyghte be the sooner pardoned,

and so god accepte theyr workes.
Yf they had made satiffaction for
that whyche is done to the congregation publikely by some no-
table punishmēt, as in the prima
tiue church was vsed to open of-
fenders, (sparkles wherof & some
traces yet remaine, when such as
haue synned in adultry go about
the churche wyth a taper in theyr
shyrtes. Or yf they had made satiffaction for restitution to manward of suche goodes as wrong-
fully is gotten, þ which true pennaunce cannot be without: Or yf
by satiffaction they had mente a
newe lyfe to make amendes to
the congregation thereby, as by
theyr euyll lyfe they dyd offende
the congregation, in whiche sence
the Apostle semeth to take that
whyche he wryteth. ii.Cor.vii.
where tholde interpretoure calleth

lest Apologian satisfactió, which
rather signifieth a defence oz an-
swerynge agayne: yf I saye, they
had taken satisfactió any of these
wayes, then they had done well,
so that the satisfaction to God
had bene left alonely to Chzyste.

Agayne, yf they had made confession eyther foz that whiche is
to god pzyuatelye, eyther foz that
whyche is to the congregation
publikelye, either foz that whych
is a free consultation, with some
one learned in gods booke, and
appoynted therunto as fyzste it
was vsed, and I wysh were now
vsed amongest vs, ether foz that
whiche is a reconciliacion one to
another, it had ben somethynge:
yea if they had made it foz fayth,
because it is a trewe demonstra-
tion of fayth, as in Paul we may
se to the Romaynes the. x. and

C.iii.   to

to the Hebrews, when he calleth
Chryste the captayne of our con-
feſſion, that is of our fayth. And
ſo confeſſours were called in the
prymitiue Church, ſuche as man
fullye dyd wytneſſe theyr fayth,
wyth the parell of theyr lyues: yf
I ſaye they hadde taken it thus,
then hadde they doone ryghte
well.

And ſo contricion, yf they had
lefte out theyr ſubtyll diſtinction
betwene it and attricion by thys
worde iuſte or full, makynge it a
hartye ſorowe for theyr ſynnes,
then we woulde neuer haue cryed oute agaynſte them therefore.
For we ſaye pennaunce hath thre
partes, contricion, yf you vnderſtande it, for a hartye ſorowyng
for ſynne. Confeſſyon, yf you vn-
derſtonde it for fayth of free pardonne in Goddes mercye by Ieſus

fus Chzyſte. And ſatiſſaction yf
you vnderſtande it not to God=
wardes(foz that onelye to Chriſt
muſte be leſte alone)but to man=
warde in reſtitucion of goodes,
wzongfully oz fraudulently got=
ten,of name hindzed by our ſſau=
ders, and in newenes oflyfe : al=
thoughe as I ſayde befoze , and
anone wyll ſhewe moze playnely
by Gods grace,that this laſte is
no parte of pennaunce in deede,
but a playne effecte oz fruyte of
true pennaunce.

I myghte here bzynge in er=
amples of theyz pennaunce,how
perilous it is to bee embzaced,
but lette the erample of theyz
graunde ſier Judas ſerue , in
whome we ſee all the partes of
their pennaunce,as they deſcribe
it,and yet notwithſtandyng was

C.iiɩ.   he

he damned. He was sory enough
as the effect shewed, he had their
contricion fully oute of the whi=
che he confessed his faute saying:
J haue betrayed innocent bloud
and there vnto he made satisfacti
on , restorynge the money he had
recepued . But yet all was but
lost, he hanged vp hym selfe , hys
bowelles burste out , and he re=
mapneth a chyld of perdition for
euer. J wolde wisshe that this ex=
ample of Judas , in whome you
see the partes of theyr pennaunce
contricion, confession, and satisfa
ction, woulde moue them to pen=
naunce, and to describe it a lytell
better, makynge hope or trust of
Gods free mercy a pece thereof,
or elles with Judas they wyll
marre all.

Perchaunce these wordes, con
tricion, confession, and Satisfa=
ction

ection were vsed as I haue expos
ded them at the first. But in that
we see so muche daunger & hurt
by vsynge them withoute expositions, eyther let vs ioyne to them
open expositions alwayes : or elles let vs not vse them at all, but
saye as I wryte, that pennaunce
is a hartye sorow for our sinnes,
a good hope or truste of pardone
thorough Christe, whyche is not
withoute an earneste purpose to
amende or a new lyfe. This pennaunce is the thynges whereto
all the scripture calleth vs , this
pennaunce do I nowe cal you al
vnto , this muste be continuallye
in vs, and not for a lent season, as
we haue thoughte. This muste
increase dayly more and more in
vs , withoute this we cannot be
saued.

Searche therfore your harts
all,

all, all swearers, blasphemers, ly
ars, flatterers, baudye oʒ ydle
talkers, gesters, bribers, couetouse, dʒonckardes, glottonnes,
whoʒemongers, theues, murthe-
rers, flaunderers, ydle lyuers,
necligente in theyʒ vocation. &c.
All suche and all other as lament
not theyʒ synnes, as hope not
in Goddes mercy foʒ pardon, as
purpose not hartelye to amende,
to leaue theyʒ swearynge, dʒon-
kennesse, whoʒedome, couetous-
nesse, ydelnesse. &c. all suche I say
shall not, noʒ cannot entre into
Goddes kyngedome, but hell fyer is pʒepared foʒ them, we-
pyngʒ and gnasshynge of teethe,
where vnto alasse I feare me berye manye will needes goo, in
that verye manye wilbe as they
haue bene, lette vs euen to the
wearynge of oure toungue to
the

the stompes, preache and praye neuer so muche to the contrarye, and that euen in the bowelles of Jesus Christe, as nowe I beseeh you all, all, all, and euerye mothers chylde, to repente and lamente youre synne, to truste in Gods mercy, and to amend your lyues.

Now me thinks you are some what astonnied, whereby I gather that presentlye you desyer this repentaunce, that is, thys sorowe, good hope, and newenesse of lyfe: the whyche that you maye the rather attayne and get to youre comfortes, as I haue goone aboute to be a meane to sturre vp (by Goodes grace) this desire of repentaunce, so through the same grace of God, wyll I go aboute now to shew you, how you may haue your desier in this behalfe.

behalfe. And fyrste concernynge
this part, namely sorow for your
synnes and hartye lamentynge
of the same.

For this (yf you desier the hauynge of it) you muste beware
that you thinke not that of youre
selues, or of your owne freewyll,
by any meanes you cā get it, you
maye easely deceaue your selues,
and mocke your selues, thinking
more of your selues then is seme-
lye.

Il good thynges, and not peces of good thinges, but all good
thinges sayeth S. James commeth from God ŷ father of light,
If therefore pennaunce be good
(as it is good) then the partes of
it be good. From God therefore
do they come, and not of our free
wyll. It is the Lorde that mor-
tifieth, that bringeth downe, that
humbleth

Jam.i.

i.Reg.ii.

humbleth sayth the scripture in
sundrye places. After thou haddest striken my thigh sayeth Ie-
rempe, I was aſhamed. Lo he
sayth, after thou haddest striken
me:and therfore prayeth he euen
the last wordes almooſe he wri-
teth: Turne vs lord and we ſhall
be turned,the whyche thing Dauyd doth very often. Wherefore,
fyrst of all,if thou wouldeſt haue
this parte of pennaunce, as for
the whole (becauſe it is goddes
gyft.) Iete.xi. ii. Timo.ii.so for
this part,go thou vnto God,and
make some lyttel prayer,as thou
canſt vnto his mercy for the same
in this or lyke sorte.

Mercifull father of our sauioure Jeſus Chryſte, becauſe I
haue ſynned and done wickedly,
and thorowe thy goodnes haue
receaued a deſire of repentaunce
wherto

Hie. xxx

Lam. v.

Actes. v.

whereto this longe sufferaunce
doth draw my hard heart. I besech thy mercy in Christ to worke
the same repentaunce in me: & by
thy spyryte, power, and grace, to
humble, mortifye, and feare my
conscyence for my synnes to saluation, that in thy tyme thou
mayeste comforte and quycken
me, thoroughe Jesus Christe thy
dearly beloued sonne. Amen. After this sort I say, or otherwyse,
as thou thynkeste good, yf thou
wylte haue this fyrste parte, contricion, or sorowe for thy synnes,
do thou begge it of God, thorow
Christe. And when thou haste
asked it, as I haue laboured to
dryue thee frome trustynge in
thy selfe, so nowe I gooe a-
boute to moue thee frome flat-
terynge of thy selfe, frome slug-
gishnes

gyftnes and negligence, to be dilygente to vse these meanes folowynge.

Unto prayer whych I would thou shouldest fyrste vse as thou canste: Secondly, get thee Gods lawe as a glasse to toote in, for in it, and by it commeth the trewe knowledge of synne, wythoute whyche knoweledge there can be no sorrowe. For howe can a man sorrowe for his synnes, whyche knoweth not his synnes ¿ As when a man is sycke, the fyrste steppe to health, is to knowe hys sicknesse, euen so to saluacion the fyrste steppe thereto, is to knowe thy dampnation due for thy synnes.

The lawe of God therefore muste be gotten, and well tooted in, that is, we muste looke in it spiri=

spirituallye, and not corporallye
or carnally as the outward word
or letter doth declare and vtter,
and so oure sauioure teacheth vs
in the. v. of Math. expoundinge
the. vi. and. vii. commaundemen
tes, not onely after the outward
dede, but also after the hearte,
makynge there the anger of the
hart a kynd of murther, lustinge
after an other mans wyfe, a kind
of adulterye.

And this is one of the differences betwene Gods lawe and
mannes lawe . That of thys
(mannes lawe I meane) I am
not condempnable, so longe as I
obserue outwardely the same.

But Goddes lawe goeth to
the roote, and to the harte, con-
dempnynge me for the inwarde
mocion althoughe outwardlye
I lyue mooste holely . As for example

ample. yf I kyll no man, though
in my heart I hate: mans law cō
dempneth me not: but otherwise
doeth gods law: And why, for it
seeth the fountayne whence the
euyl doeth spryng, If hatred wer
taken out of the hearte, loftinesse
in lookes, detraction in tonge, &
murther by hand, could neuer en
sue. yf lustinge were out of the
heart, curiositie in countenaunce
wantónes in wordes, thē baudie
boldnesse, in body would not ap-
peare. In that therfore this outwarde euyll springes out of the
inwarde corruption: seynge gods
lawe also is a lawe of libertie, as
sayth S. James: And spirituall Iam. ii.
as sayth S. Paul: Perfectly and Ro.vii.
spiritually, it is to be vnderstand,
yf we wyll truelye come to the
knowledge of our synnes. For of
this inwarde corruption, reason
D.i.   knoweth

knoweth but litle oʒ nothinge : J
had not knowē ſayth Paul, ẏ luſ-
ting (whiche to reaſon, ꝗ to them
which are gyded only by reaſō, is
thoughte but a trifle) J had not
knowen ſayth he, this luſtinge to
haue ben ſin, if ẏ law had not ſaid
Nō cōcupiſces, thou ſhalt not luſt.

¶To the knowledge therefoʒe of
our ſinne (ẃout which we cannot
repent oʒ be ſoʒy foʒ our ſinne) let
vs ſecondly gette gods lawe as a
glaſſe to toote in: ꝗ that not onlye
litterally, outwardly, oʒ partely,
but alſo ſpiritually, inwardlye, ꝗ
thʒoughly : let vs cōſidʒe the hart
ꝗ ſo ſhall we ſee the foule ſpottes
we are ſtayned withal, at least inwardly, wherby we ẏ rather may
be moued to harti ſoʒow ꝗ ſighig
foʒ as ſ. Auſten ſaith it is a glaſ
whiche feareth no body : but euen
loke what a one ẏ art ſo it paintes
the

the oute . In the lawe we see it is
a foule spot not to loue the Lorde
our God wal(al I say)our heart
soule, power, might & strength, &
that cótinually, In the law it is a
foule spotte, not onely to make to
our selues anye grauen ymage or
similitude, to bowe therto. &c. but
also not to frame our selfes whol
ly after the ymage wherto we are
made not to bow to it, to worship
it. In the law we se ꝥ it is a foule
spot, not onlye to take gods name
in vain: but also not earnestli, har
tely; & euen cótinually to cell vpó
his name only, to geue thákes vn
to him, to beleue, to publishe, & to
liue his holy word. In gods law
we se it is a foule spot to our soules, not only to be an opé propha-
ner of ꝥ saboth day: but also not to
rest fró our own words & works
that the lord might both speake &

D.ii.   worke

worke in vs, & by vs:not to heare
his holy worde:not to communi=
cate his sacramentes,not to geue
occasion to others to holynes, by
our example in godlye workes &
reuerent esteming of the ministe=
rie of his worde.

In Gods law we see it a foule
spot to our soules not onlye to be
an opē disobeyer of our parents,
magistrates, maysters, and such
as be in anye auctoritie ouer vs:
but also not to honour suche,euen
in our heartes, not to geue than=
kes to God for them , not to pray
for them to ayde, to helpe , or re=
leue them,to beare wyth their in=
firmities.&c. In Gods lawe we
see it a foule spotte in oure soules
not onlye to be a manqueller in
hatered, malyce , proude lookes,
bragges,backbiting,raylinge,or
bodely slaughter : but also not to
loue

loue oure neyghbours, yea oure
enemies, euen in our hartes, and
to declare $ same in al our iesture
wordes and workes. In Gods
law we see it a foule spot to oure-
soules, not onelye to be a whore-
monger in lusting in our heartes
in wanton loking, in vncleane or
wanton talking, in actuall doing
vnhonestly with our neyghbors
wife, doughter, seruant, &c. but
also not to be chast, sobre, tempe-
rate in harte, lokes, tonge, appa-
tell, deedes, and to helpe others
there vnto accordinglye. &c. In
Gods law we see it is a foule spot
to our soules, not onely in harte
to couet, in loke, or worde, to flatter, lye colour. &c. in dede to take
away any thing whiche pertayneth to another: but also in heart
countenaúce, word & dede, not to
kepe, saue, and defend that which

per-

pertayneth to thy neyghboure as
thou wouldest thine own.

Jn Gods law we maye see it a
foule spot, not only to lie, oz beare
false witnes agaynst any mã but
also not to haue as greate care
ouer thy neyghboures name, as
ouer thine owne. Sinne in gods
law it is (we may se) as foule spot
not only to consent to euil lust, oz
carnall desyzes, but euen the very
natural oz carnal lustes & desires
thẽ selues, foz so J may cal thẽ na
turail it self, beyng now so cozrup
ted as self loue, & many such like,
by reason wherof, J trow ther is
none, that toteth well herein, but
though he be blameles to þ wozld
& fayze to þ shewe, yet certaynely
inwardly, his face is foule arated
& so shamful saucie mãgie, pocked
& skabbed, þ he cãnot, but be sozy,
at the cõtẽplaciõ therof: & that so
muche

much moze by how much he con-
tinueth to loke in this glas accoz
dingly. And thus much cōcernig
the secōd mean to ꝑ stirring vp of
sozowe foz our sinne:ꝑ nexte vnto
pzaier,we shuld tote in gods law
spiritually: ꝑ which toting yf we
vse w pzaier(as I said)let vs not
Doubt,but at ꝑ lēgth,gods spirit
wil wozke,as now to such as beleue, (foz to ꝑ vnbeleuers al is in
vayn:Their eyes ar starke blind
they can see nothynge)to suche as
beleue(I say)I trust somthing is
done euen already. But yf nether
by pzayer noz by tooting in gods
lawe spiritually,as yet thy harde
vnbeleuing hart fealeth no sozow
noz lamēting foz thy sinne:Third
ly loke vpon ꝑ tagge tied to gods
law,foz as to mās lawes,there is
a tagge tied,ꝑ is a penaltie. So
is there to Goddes lawe a tagge

tyed, that is a penaltie: and that
no small one, but suche a greate
one, as can not, but make vs to
caste our curriseshe tayles betwene
our legges, yf we beleue it, for all
is in vayne, yf we be faythles not
to beleue before we feele.

Gal. iii. This tage is Gods maledictió
or curse, maledictus omnis (sayth
it) qui nõ permanet in omnibus quæ
scripta sunt in libro legis vt faciat
eam, Loe, accursed (saith he) is all
no accepttó, al sayth god which có
tinueth not, in al things (for he ꝑ
is giltie of one is giltie of ꝑ whole
sayeth S. James) In al thinges
therefore, (sayeth the holy ghost)
which are writté in ꝑ boke of the
lawe to do them: he sayeth not to
heare them, te talke of them, to
dispute of them, but to doe them.
Who is he now that doth these?
Rara auis, fewe such byrdes, yea
none

none at all. For all are gone oute of the way, though not outward-lye by word or dede, yet inward-ly at the least, by defaulte & wan-tinge of that whiche is requyred: so that a chylde of one nyghtes age is not pure, but (by reason of byrth sinne) in daunger of Gods malediction. Much more then we which halas haue dronke in ini-quitie as it were water, as Job sayeth : but yet halas we quake not. Tell me nowe good brother why do you so lightlye consyder Gods curse, that for your synnes past you are so careles as though you had made a couenaunt with death and damnation as the wic-ked dyd in Esayes time: what is Gods curse? At the popes curse with boke, bell, & candle, oh howe trembled we, whiche harde it but onelye, though the same was not direc-

Job.xv.

directed vnto vs, but vnto others
to this Goddes curſſe, whyche is
incomparable, moꝛe fel, ⁊ impoꝛta-
ble, ⁊ is directed, yea hãging ouer
vs al, by reaſon of our ſinnes, halas how careles ar we? Oh faith=
les harde hartes . Oh Iezabels
geſtes, rocked ⁊ laid a ſlepe in her
bed, Oh wicked wꝛetches, whych
being come into the depe of ſinne
do cõtẽpne theſame, Oh ſoꝛowles
ſinners and ſhameles chꝛinking
harlots, Is not ꝑ anger of a king
death? ⁊ is the anger of the kinge
of all kinges a matter to be ſo
lightlye regarded , as we doe re-
gard it, which(for our ſinnes)are
ſo recheles ꝑ we ſlug ⁊ ſlepe it out?
As ware melteth away at ꝑ heat
of the fyꝛe(ſaith Dauid)ſo do the
wicked periſh, at ꝑ face oꝛ counte-
naũce of ꝑ loꝛd:Yf dearly beloued
his face be ſo terrible, and intolle=
rable

Apoc. iii.

rable foz sinners,and the wicked:
What trowe we his had is:At the
face oz apearing of gods anger,ÿ
earth trembleth : but we earth,
earth,yea stones,yzõ,flintes, trēble nothinge at all:yf we will not
trēble in hearing,wo vnto vs foz
then shal we be crashed a peces in
feeling: yf a lyon roze the beastes
quake,but we are wozsse thẽ beastes,which quake nothing at the
rozing of the lion,I meane ÿ lozd
of hostes. And why: because the
cursse of God, hardenes of heart,
Thzeno.iii.is already fallẽ vpon
vs,oz els we could not but lamẽt
& trēble foz our synnes, yf not foz
the shame and foulenes thereof:
yet at the least foz the maledictiõ
and cursse of God,whiche hāgeth
ouer vs foz our synnes.

     Lozde be mercyfull vnto vs
foz thy Chzistes sake, and spare
                                   vs

vs in thyne anger, remembꝛe thy mercy towardes vs. Amen.

And thus muche foꝛ the thyꝛde thing to the mouing of vs to soꝛow foꝛ oure sinnes (that is foꝛ ẏ tagge tied to Gods law) I mean foꝛ the malediction and curſſe of God.

But yf our heartes be ſo heard that thoꝛow theſe we yet fele not harty soꝛow foꝛ our ſynnes: Let vs fourthlye ſet befoꝛe vs examples paſt, and pꝛeſent, old ⁊ new: that therby the holy ſpirite may be effectual to woꝛke in his tyme, this woꝛke of soꝛowing foꝛ oure ſinne.

Loke vpon Godes anger foꝛ ſynne in Adam and Eue: foꝛ eating a pece of an apple. Were not thei the deareſt creatures of god caſt oute of Paradyſe: were not they ſubiect to moꝛtalitie, traueil
labour

labour.&c.was not the earth accursed for theyr sinnes? Doe not
we all,men in laboure,women in
traueling with chylde, and all in
death,mortalitie,& miserie, euen
in thys lyfe feele the same? And
was god so angry for theyr sinne
and he being the same God, wyll
he saye nothinge to vs for oures,
halas muche more horrible then
the eating once of one pece of an
apple?

In the tyme of Noe and Lot, Gen. vi.
Gen.rix.
God destroyed the whole worlde
with water,and the cities of So
doma and Gomorra, Seboim&
Adamah with fyre and brymston
from heauen , for theyr synnes:
Namely for theyr whoredomes,
pryde, idlenes, vnmercifulnes to
the poore,tyrannie.&c. In whych
wrath of God euen the verye ba-
bes,byrdes,foules,fisshes,herbes
trees

trees, and graffe perished. And thinke we that nothinge wylbe spokē to vs, muche worse & more abhominable thē they: for al mē may see yf they will ý the whore-dōs, pride, vnmercifulnes, tirannie. &c. of England far passeth in this age, any age ý euer was before. Lots wyfe loking back was turned into a salt stone, & wil our loking back againe, yea our running back agayne to our wickednes do vs not hurt: yf we were not alredy more blind thē bettels we woulde bluffe. Pharaohys heart was hardened so ý no myracle could conuert him: yf oures were any thing softe, we woulde begin to sobbe.

Gen. rix.

Iofue & Caleb.

Of syre hundreth thousande men, alonely but twayne entred into the land of promyse, because they had tē times synned agaynst

the

the Lorde, as he him selfe sayeth.
Num. riiii. And trow we ý God
wil not sweare in his wrath, that
we shall neuer entre into his rest,
whiche haue sinned so manye ten
times as we haue toes & fingers,
yea heares of our heades & bear-
des I fere me, & yet we passe not.

The mã that sware, Leu. rriiii.
and he that gathered stickes on
the Saboth day. Num. rb. were
stoned to death : but we thynke
our swearing is no sinne, our bib-
bing, rioting, yea whorehunting
on the Saboth day, pleaseth god
or els we woulde some thynge a-
mende our maners.

Helias negligence in correc- i. Reg. iiï
ting his sones, nipped his neck in
two: But oures whiche pãper vp
oure children lyke puppets, wyll
putte vs to no plounge:

Helias sonnes for disobeying
theyr

theyr fathers monicion brought
ouer them godes vengaūce, and
wyl our stubbernes do nothing.

iii. Reg.
rri. rrii.
Saule his malice to Dauid, A-
chabs displeasur agaynste Na-
both, brought theyr bloud to the
iiii. kin.
rri.
grounde for dogges to eate, yea
their cheldren wer hanged vp &
iiii. kin. r
slayne for this geare, but we con-
tinue in malice, enuie, & murther,
as though we were able to wage
warre wyth the Lord.

ii. kin. ri
rii. riii.
rvi. rv.
Dauids adultrie with Beth-
sabe was vysyted on the chylde
borne, on Dauides daughter, defyled by her brother, and on hys
chyldren one slaying another, on
hys wyues defyled by hys owne
sonne, on him selfe dryuen out of
hys realme in his olde age, and
otherwise also, although he most
hartely repēted his sinne: but we
are more dere vnto god thē Dauid

nid, whiche yet was a man after
gods owne hart, or els we could
not but tremble, and begynne to
repent.

The riche glottonnes gaye
paunche fyllynge, what did it? it
brought hym to hel, and haue we
a plackarde that God wyll do no
thynge to vs.

Achams subtyll theft prouoked
Gods anger against all Israell:
and our subteltie, yea open extor
cion is so fyne and politike, that
God cannot espye it.

Giezi his couetousnes brou=
ghte it not the lepzosy vpon him,
and on all hys sede. Judas also
hanged hym selfe: But the co=
uetousnes of Englande is of
an other cloathe and coulloure.
well, yf it were so, the same tay=
ler wyll cutte it accozdynge=
lye.

Lu. xbi.

Joſu. bii

iiii. re. b.

Act. i.

E. i.   Ana=

Act.v. Anania and Saphira by ly-
inge, lynked to them sodayne
death: but oures nowe prolon-
geth oure lyfe the longer, to laste
in eternall death.

Da. xiii. The false wytnesses of the
two Iudges against Susanna,
lighte on their owne partes, and
so wyll ours do at length.

But what go I about to a-
uouche aunciente exaumples,
where daylye experience doeth
teach. The sweat the other year,
the stormes the winter folowing
wyl vs to way them in the same
ballaunces.

The hangynge, and kyllynge
of men them selues, whiche are
alas to ryfe in all places, requier
vs to register them in the same
rolles.

At the least in Chyldren, in-
fauntes, and such like, which yet
can

can not vtter synne by worde or
dede, we see Goddes anger a-
gaynste Synne, in punysshynge
them by syckenes, death, mys-
happe or otherwyse so playnely
that we cannot but grone and
grount agayne, in that we a lyttell more haue gusshed oute thys
geare gorgeously in worde and
dede.

And here with me a litel loke
on gods anger, yet so fresshe, that
we cannot but smell it, although
we stop our noses neuer so much
I praye God we smel it not more
fresshe hereafter. I meane it forsoth (for I know you loke for it)
in our dere late souereigne lorde
the kings maieste. you all know
he was but a childe in yeares:
defyled he was not with notori-
ous offences. Defiled o he naye
rather adorned w so many good
ly gyftes,

and wonderfull qualities as neuer prynce was from the begynnyng of ye worlde. Shuld I speke of his wysedome: of his rypenes in iudgement: of his learning: of his Godlye zeale, heroical heart, fatherly care for hys commons, norcely solicitude for religion:&c naye so manye thinges are to be spoken in commendatiō of gods exceedyng graces in this childe, that as Salust wryteth of Chartage I had rather speak nothing then to lytel, in ye to much is to litle. This gift God gaue vnto vs Englych men, before all nacions vnder the sonne, and that of his exceedynge loue towardes vs. But alas and welawaye for our vnthankefulnes sake, for our sinnes sake, for our carnalitie, and prophan liuing, gods anger hath touched not only ye body, but also

the

the mynde of our king, by a long
sycknes, and at length hath take
hym awaye by death, death, cru-
ell death, fearful death, death. &c.

Oh if Gods iudgement be be-
gon on him, which as he was the
chiefest, so I thinke the holiest, &
godliest in ý realme of England, Psalm.
alas what wyl it be on vs, whose xxxviii.
synnes are ouer growne so oure
heades, that they are climed vp
into heauen.

I praye you my good brethren
knowe that gods anger for oure
sinnes towardes vs cannot but
be great, yea to fel, in that we se it
was so great, that our good king
coulde not beare it. What folo-
wed to Iewry after the death of
Iosias? God saue England, and
geue vs repētaunce, my hart will
not suffer me to tary longer herein. I trow this wyll thruste oute

some

some teares of repentaunce,

Yf therefore to prayer for gods
feare, the tootynge in gods glas
and the tagge thereto, wyll not
burste open thy blockysh hearte,
yet I trowe the tossynge to and
fro, of these examples, and spe-
cyally of our late kinge, and this
trouble some tyme, wyll tomble
some teares oute of thyne hearte,
yf thou styll praye for Gods spirite accordynglye. For who arte
thou (thynke alwayes wyth thy
selfe) that G O D shoulde spare
thee, more then they, whose examples thou haste harde? what
feendes haste thou? were not of
these, Kynges, Prophetes, Apostles, Learned, and commen of
holye stockes? I deceaue my
selfe, thynke thou with thy selfe,
yf I beleue G O D, beynge the
same

same G O D that he was, wyll
spare me, whose wyckednesse is
no lesse, but much more then some
of theyrs : he hateth synne nowe,
as muche as euer he dydde : the
longer he sparethe, the greater
vengeaūce wyll fall. The derper
he draweth his bowe, the soorer
wyll the shatte pearce.

But yf yet thy harte be so
hardened, that all thys geare
wyll not moue thee : Suerlye
thou arte in a berye euyll estate,
and remedy now knowe I none.
What sayde I none: knowe I
none: yes, yet there is one whiche
is suresbye as they saye, to serue
yf anye thynge will serue, you
loke to knowe what this is:
Forsooth the passion and death
of Iesus C H R I S T E. you
knowe the cause whye Chryste

became

became man, and suffered as he
suffered, was the synnes of hys
people that he myghte saue them
from the same. Consider ÿ great-
nes of the soore, J meane synne,
by the greatenesse of the Surgion, and of the salue. Who was
the Surgion: no Aungell, no
sainct, no Archaungell, no power
no creature in heuē, nor in earth,
but onely he by whom al thinges
were made, all thynges are ruled
also: euen Gods owne Deatlyng,
and onely beloued Sonne, becō-
mynge man.

Oh what a great thinge is this
that coulde not be doone by the
aungels, archaūgels, potestates,
powers, or all the creatures of
God, wythout his owne Sonne,
who yet muste nedes be thruste
out of heauen, as a man woulde
saye,

faye, to take oure nature and become man? Here haue ye the fur-
gion, greate was the cure that
thys mightye LORDE toke in
bande.

Nowe, what was the falue?
Foꝛfoth dere geare, and of many
compofitions, I cannot recite al,
but rather mufte leaue it to your
harty confiderations. Thꝛee and
thyꝛtye yeares was he curynge
oure foꝛe: he fought it earneftlye,
by faftynge, watchynge, pꝛayinge.⁊c.

The fame nyghte he was be- mat.rrb
trayed, I read how bufy he was Lu.rrii.
aboute a playfter in the garden,
when he lying flat on the ground
pꝛayinge wyth teares: and that
of bloud not a fewe, but fo many
as dydde flowe downe on the
grounde agayne, cryinge on
this foꝛte: Father fayeth he, yf it
be

be possible , lette thys cuppe departe frome me , that is , yf it be possible els mankyndes synnes cannebe taken awaye , graunte that it maye be so. Thou hardest Moyses cryinge for the ydolaters: Thou hardeste Lot for the zoarites: Samuell, Dauyd, and manye other for the Israelites, and deare Father , I onelye am thyne owne sonne, as thou haste sayde , in whome thou arte well pleased , wylte thou not heare me: I haue by the space of thre and thyrty yeares done alwayes thy wyll, I haue so humbled my selfe that I woulde become an abiecte amongeste men to obeye thee : Therefore deare father yf it be possible graunte my request, saue mankynde nowe wythoute any further laboure. Salues, or

plaisters

playſters: But yet (ſayth he) not
as I wyll, but as thou wylte.

But ſyʒ what harde heithou-
ughe he ſweate bloude and water in makynge hys playſter foʒ
oure ſoʒe of ſynne, yet it framed
not: twyſe he cryed wythoute
comfoʒte: yea, thoughe to com-
foʒt hym, GOD ſente an Aungell, we yet knowe that thys
Playſter was not alowed foʒ ſufficiente, vntyll herevnto Chʒyſte
Jeſus was betrayed, foʒſaken of
all hys Diſcyples, foʒſwoʒne of
hys dearelye beloued, bounde
lyke a thefe, belyed on, buffeted,
whypped, ſkourged, crowned
with thoʒnes, derided, crucified,
racked, nayled, hanged vppe betwene twoo theues, curſed and
rayled vppon, mocked in myſe-
rye, and hadde geuen vppe the
ghoſte,

ghoste then bowed downe the
heade of Chryste, that is GOD
the father, whyche is the heade of
Chrste. i. Corinth. ri. then alowed he the playster to be sufficient
and good for the healynge of our
sore, whych is sinne. Now wolde
GOD abyde our breath, because
the stincke, that is dampnation
or gyltynesse was taken awaye,
by the swete savour of the breath
of this lambe, thus offered once
for all.

So that here dearelye beloued, we as in a glasse, maye se to
the broosynge of oure blockyshe
harde heartes, Goddes greate
iudgemente and anger agaynste
synne: The Lorde of Lordes,
the kynge of kynges, the bryght-
nes of Goddes glorye, the sonne
of GOD, the dearelynge of
hys father, in whome he is well
pleased

pleased, hangeth betwene twoo
theues, crpinge for thee and me, Psalm.
and for vs al, My God, my god, xxii.
why haste thou forsaken me?
Oh harde heartes that we haue
whych make tuttes for syn:looke
on this toote in the very harte of
Chryste, pearced wyth a speare,
where in thou mayeste see and
reade Goddes horrible anger for
sinne:woo to thy hard harte that
pearsed it.

And thus muche for the fyrste
parte of repentaunce, I meane
for the meanes of workynge
contricion. Fyrste vse prayer, thē
looke on G O D D E S lawe,
thyrdely, se hys curse, fourthlye,
sette exaumples of hys anger:
and laste of all, sette before thee,
the death of Chryste, frome thys
and prayer cease not, tyll thou
feele some hartye sorowe for thy

Sinne. The whiche when thou
fealeste, then laboure for the o-
ther parte, that is fayth on this
sorte.

As fyrste in contrition I wil-
led thee not to truste to thy free
wyll for that taininge of it, so do
I wyll thee in this. Fayth is so
farre frome the reache of mannes free wyll: that to reasonne
it is playne folyshnes. Therefore
thou muste fyrste go to G O D,
whose gyfte it is: thou muste I
saye, gette thee to the father of
mercye, whose woorke it is,
John the syxth, that as he hathe
brought þ downe by contrition,
and humbled thee, so he woulde
geue the fayth, rayse thee vppe,
Collossians.ii,and exalte thee.
On this manner therfore, with
the Apostles, and the poore man
in the Gospell that cryed, Lorde
encrease

encrease oure fayeth, LORD helpe me vnbeleife, praye thou and saye.

O mercyfull GOD, and deare father of oure Lorde and sauyoure Iesus Christ, in whom as thou arte well pleased, so hast thou commaunded vs to heare hym, forasmuche as he often biddeth vs, to aske of thee, and ther to prompseth that thou wylte heare vs, and graunte vs that whyche in hys name we shall aske of thee: Loe gracious father I am bolde to begge of thy mercye thoroughe thy Sonne Iesus Christe, one sparckle of true fayth and certayne perswasion of thy goodnes, and loue towardes me in Christe, where throughe I beynge assewred of the pardonne of all my sinnes, by the mercyes of CHRIST thy sonne,

Sonne, may be thankful to thee, loue thee, and serue thee, in holynes & rightuousnes al the dayes of my lyfe.

On this sorte I saye, or other wyse, as GOD shall moue thee, praye thou fyrste of all, and looke for thy request at GODDES hande withoute any doubtynge, thoughe forthwyth thou feeleste not the same : for oftentymes we haue thynges of GOD geuen vs, longe before we feele them as we woulde do. Nowe vnto thys prayer vse thou these meanes folowynge.

After prayer for fayth, whiche I woulde shoulde be firste: Secondlye because the same spryngeth oute of the hearynge, not of Masses, Mattens, Cannons, councels doctours, decrees, but out of the hearing of gods word:

Get

Get the gods word, but not that
part whiche serueth speciallye to
contricion, that is the lawe, but
the other part which serueth spe
cially to consolacion, and certayn
perswasiō of gods loue towards
the, that is the Gospel or pubica-
tion of Gods mercy in Christ, I
meane the free promyses.

But here thou must knowe, ꝑ
there is two kyndes of promises
one which are properly of ꝑ law,
another which ar properly of the
Gospell.

In the promyses of the lawe,
we may in dede beholde Goddes
mercy, but so that it hāgeth ouer
the condicion of our worthynes,
as yf thou loue the Lord with al
thy hearte, &c. thou shalt fynde
mercy.

This kynd of promyses though
it declare vnto vs Goddes loue,

which

which promiseth where he endeth
not, yet vnto him that feleth not
Christe, whiche is the ende of the
lawe, they are so farre from côfor
tinge, that vtterly with the law,
they bringe manne to greate dis-
payre, so greatly we are corrupt:
for none so loueth G O D as he
oughte to doe.   From these
therefore get the to the other promyses of the Gospel in which we
may see suche plentie and franke
liberalite of Gods goodnes, that
we can not, but be muche com-
forted, though we haue very depely synned.

For these promyses of the gospell doe not hange on the condicion of oure worthynesse as the
promyses of the law do: but they
depende and hange on Goddes
trueth, that as G O D is true, so
they can not, but be perfourmed
                                    to

to al the which lay holde on them
bi faith, I had almost said which
cast them not away by vnbelefe.

Marke in them therfore two
thinges, nameli, that as wel they
ar free promyses, without anye
condiciō of our worthines, as also that they are vniuersal, offered
to al, (all I saye) which are not so
stubborne as to kepe styll, theyr
handes, whereby they shoulde re-
ceaue this almesse in theyr boso-
mes by vnbeliefe: As concerning
infantes and children you know
I now speake not but cōcerning
such as be of yeres of discrecion,
And now you loke that I should
geue you a tast of these promyses
whiche are both free and vniuersall, excepting none but suche, as
excepte them selues   Well you
shall haue cne oz two foz a saye.

In the thyrde of John sayeth
our Sauiour: so God the Father
loued the worlde, that he woulde
geue his dearling, his owne only
sonne, that all that beleue in hym
should not perish, but haue euer-
lasting lyfe. Lo syr, he sayeth not
that some might haue lyfe: but al
sayth he, And what all: all ŷ loue
him wyth all theyr heartes: all ŷ
haue lyued a godly lyfe: naye, all
ŷ beleue in him, all thoughe thou
hast liued a most wicked and horrible lyfe, yf nowe thou beleue in
him, thou shalte be saued. Is not
this swete geare:

Agayne sayth Christ. Mat. xi
come vnto me all you that labor,
and are laden, and I will refresh
you. Let vs a little looke on thys
letter: come vnto me. Who shuld
come Lord: Priestes, Holy men,
Monkes, Freres, yea coblers,
tinkers

tinkers, whozes, theues, murthe=
rets also, yf they lamente theyz
sinnes. Come vnto me sayth he,
all ye that labour and are laden,
that is, which ar afrayd foz your
sinnes: And what wilte thou doe
Lozde? and J wyll refresche you
sayth he.

Oh what a thinge is this: and
J wyll refresche you: wote you
who spake thys? he that neuer *i. Pet. ii.*
tolde lye, he is the trueth), there
was neuer gyle founde in hys
mouth: and now wyl he be vntru
to the good bzother, whiche arte
sozye foz thy greuous sinnes? no
fozsoth? Heauen and earth shall
passe and perishe, but his woozde *Math. xxiiii.*
shall neuer fayle.

Sainct Paule sayth. i. Tim. ii
God woulde haue all men saued:
lo he excepteth none. And to Ti=
tus. ii. the grace of God bzingeth
F. iii. salua=

saluacion to all mē. As frō Adam all haue rece?ued sinne to dampnation: so by Christ al haue grace offced to saluacion, yf they reiect not the same, I speake not nowe of infantes I saie: noz I nede not to enter into the matter of predestinacion, In preachinge of repentaūce, I would gather wher I could with Christ.

As surely as I lyue sayth god I wyll not the death of a synner. Arte thou a synner? yea. Lo god sweareth he wyll not thy deathe, howe canste thou nowe perishe? Consyder wyth thy selfe what profyte shouldeste thou haue to beleue this to be true to others, yf not to thy selfe also. Sathan doeth so: Rather consyder wyth Peter, that the promyse of saluacion pertayneth not only to them which

Ezec. iii.

whyche are nye, that is, to suche Actu̇. ii.
as are fallen a lyttle: but also to
all whome the LORDE hath
called, be they neuer so farre of.
Loe nowe by me the Lorde calleth thee thou manne, thou woman, that art very farre of. The
promyse therfore pertayneth to
thee, nedes muste thou be saued,
excepte thou wyth Sathan saye, ii.tim.ii.
GOD is false: and yet yf thou
do so, GOD is faithful, and can
not denye him selfe: as thou shalt
feele by hys plages in hell for soo
dishonoringe God to thynke that
he is not true.

Wyll he be founde false nowe:
the matter hangeth not on thy
worthynesse, but it hangeth on
Gods truth. Clap hold on it, and
I warrante thee, Chryste is the
propiciation of oure synnes, yea

yea for the synnes of the whole
worlde beleue this man, I know

Lu. rbi.
Mar. ir.

thou beleuest it : saye therefore in
thy hearte styll, Domine adauge
mihi fidē, lorde increase my fayth

John. rr

Lord help my vnbelefe. Blessed
are they whiche see not (by reason
this geare) but yet beleue. Hope
man past al hope, as Abrahā dyd
Roma. iiii.

And thus muche for a taste of
these promyses which are euerye
where, not onlye in the new testa-
ment, but also in the olde. Reade
the last ende of Leuiticum. rrbi.
The Prophete Esay from the. rl
Chapt. in the. rrr. sayth he, God
tarrieth loking for thee, to shewe
the mercy, reade the. ii. Regum.
rriiii. Psalm. rrriii. Joel. ii. ꝛc.

Howe beit, yf thys geare wyll
not serue, yf yet thou fealeste no
fayth, no certayne perswasion of
Gods

Gods loue: then vnto prayer, and
diligent consyderinge of the free
and vniuersall promyses of the
Gospell.

Thyrdely set before the, those
benefites, which god hath to fore
geuen thee, and presently geueth
thee. Consyder how he hath made
the a manne, or a woman, whych
myghte haue made the a toode, a
dogge, And why did he this? bee
rely because he loued the: & trow=
est thou that if he loued the, when
thou wast not, to make the such a
one, as he moste graciouslye hath
made y, wil he not trowest thou
now loue the, beynge his handye
worke? doeth he hate anye thinge
that he made? is there vnablenes
with him? Doth he loue for a daye
and so fare wel? no forsoth, he lo= Job. riii
ueth to thende, his merye endu= Psalm.
reth for euer. Say therfore wyth lrrvii.

Job

Job, Operi manum tuarum porri-
ge dexteram to the woorke of thy
hand, put thy helping hand.

Agayne hath he not made thee
a Christian man or woman, wher
yf he would, he might haue made
thee a Turke or Paynim: This
thou knoweste he dydde of loue.
And doest thou thinke his loue
is lessonede yf thou lamente thy
synne: is his hande shortened for
helpinge thee. Can a womanne
forgette the chylde of her wombe:
and thoughe she shoulde do it, yet
wyll not I forgette thee sayeth the
Lordes.

He hath geuen thee limmes,
to see, heare, go. &c. He hath geué
thee wytte, reason, discretion. &c.
He hath longe spared thee, and
borne wyth thee, when thou neuer purposedst to repent, & now
thou repenting, wyll he not geue
the

thee mercy: wherfore doeth he
geue the to lyue at this presente:
to heare me to speake this, and
me to speake this: but of loue to
vs all. Oh therfore let vs praye
him that he would adde to thys,
that we mighte beleue these loue
tokens, that he loueth vs, and in
deede he wyll doe it. Lorde open
our eyes, in thy gyftes to see thy
gracious goodnesse. Amen.

But to tarrye in this I wyll
not: euery man let him consyder
Gods benefytes, paste, and pre=
sente, publyke and priuate, spiri=
tuall and corporall, to the confir=
minge of hys fayth concerninge
the promyses of the Gospell, for
the pardone of his synnes.   I
wyll nowe go to shewe you a
fourth meane to confirme youre
fayth of thys geare, euen by ex=
amples.

Of

Of these there are in the scrip-
tures very manye, as also daylye
experience doth diuerslye teache
the same, yf we were diligente to
obserue thynges accordynglye,
wherefore I wyll be more brefe
Gen.iii. herein, hauinge respecte to tyme,
whych stealeth fast awaye.

Adam in Paradyse transgres-
sed greuously as the paynful pu-
nishment, which we al as yet doe
feele, proueth, yf nothinge els else.
Thoughe by reason of his synne
he displeased God, sore and ran
awaye from God, for he woulde
haue hyd him selfe, yea he would
haue made God the causer of his
synne, in that he gaue hym such a
mate, so farre was he frõ askinge
mercye yet all this not withstandinge, GOD turned hys fearce
wrath nether vpõ him, nor Eue,
which also requyred not mercye,
but

but vpon the serpente Sathan: Promysing vnto them a sede Iesus Christe, by whom they at the lenght shoulde be delyuered: In token whereof, though they were caste oute of Paradyse, for theyr nurture, to serue in sorow, which woulde not serue in ioye, yet he made thē apparell to couer theyr bodies, a visible sacramente and tokē of his inuisible loue & grace, concerning theyr soules.

Yf God was so merciful to Adam, whych so sore brake hys cōmaundemēt, and rather blamed God, then asked mercy, trowreste thou oh man, that he wyll not be mercyful to the, whiche blameste thy selfe and desyrest pardon.

To Cayn he offered mercy, if he woulde haue asked it: What haste thou done sayeth God: the voyce of thy brothers bloude cryeth

Gen. iiii

cryeth vnto me, out of the earth:
Oh mercyfull Lord (Chuld Cayn
haue sayd) I cōfesse it. But halas
he dyd not so: And therfore sayde
God. Now, that is, in that thou
despysest not mercy, now I say: be
thou accursed. &c. Lo so the re-
probate he offced mercy, and will
he denye it thee whiche arte hys
chylde.

Gene .ix Noah dyd not he synne and
was drōke: Good Lot also bothe
Gen .xix in Sodome dissembled a lyttle
wyth the Aungels, prolonginge
the tyme, & out of Sodom he fell
Gene. very foule: as did Iudas, and the
xxxviii. & Patriarches, agaynste Ioseph,
xxxvii but yet I wene they foūd mercy.

Moyses, Myriam, Aaron,
Num.xi. though they tombled a little, yet
receaued they mercye: yea the
people in the wyldernesse often
synned & displeased God so that
he

he was purposed to haue destroy
ed them:let me alone sayth he to   Er.rrrit
Moyses, that J maye destroye
them,but Moyses dyd not lette
hym alone,for he prayed styll for
them, and therefore God spared
them.yf the people were spared
throughe Moyses prayer, they
not praing with him, but rather
worshipping theyr golden calfe,
eatinge,drinkinge,and makinge
ioly good cheare:why shooldest
thou doubte , whether God wyll
be mercyfull to thee: hauynge as
in dede thou hast,one muche bet-
ter then Moyses to pray for thee   Ro. viii.
and with thee,euen Jesus Chzist
who sytteth on the right hand of
his father and prayeth for vs,be-   Hebr .iii
ing no lesse faithful in his fathers
house the church the moses was
in the Sinagoge.Dauid ẏ good   ii.Re.ri.
Kyng, had a foule foyle,when he
                    committed

committed whoredoin, with hys
faythfull seruauntes wyfe Beth-
sabe, where vntohe added also a
mischeuous murder, causing her
husband hys most faythfull soul-
diour Urye to be slayne with an
honest company of his most vali-
aunt mē of warre, and that with
the swearde of the vncircumcis-
sed. In this his synne thoughe
a great whyle he laye a slepe(as
many do now a dayes, god geue
them wynne waking) thinking
that by his sacrifices he offered,
all was well, God was content:
yet at length when the Prophet
by a parable had opened the poke
and brought hym in remēbraūce
of his owne synne in such sorte, ŷ
he gaue iudgement agaynst hym
self, thē quaked he, his sacryfices
hadde no more taken awaye his
sinnes, then our syr Johns tren-
tals.

talles, and waggynge of his fyn-
gers ouer the heades of luche as
lye a slepe in theyr synnes, out of
the whyche when they are awa-
ked, they wyll well se, it is nether
masse, nor mattens, blessyng, nor
crossyng wyll serue: then (I say)
he cryed out sayinge, peccaui do-
mino, I haue synned sayeth he a-
gaynst my Lorde, and good god
whyche hath doone so muche for
me, I caused in dede Urye to be
kylled, I haue synned, I haue sin
ned, what shall I doo? I haue
synned and am worthye of eternall dampnatió. But what sayth
God by his Prophete: Dominus
(sayth he) transtulit peccatum tuũ
non morieris, the Lorde hath taken awaye thy synnes thou shalt
not dye. Oh good God, he sayed
but peccaui, I haue synned, but

yet from his harte, and not from
the lyppes onelye, as Pharao &
Saule dyd, and incontinentelye
he heareth: Thou shalte not dye:
the Lorde hath taken awaye thy
synnes , or rather hath layde
them vpon an other, yea transla-
ted them vppon the backe of hys
sonne Iesus Chryste, who bare
them , and not onelye them , but
thyne and myne also , yf that we
wyll nowe crye, but from oure
hartes, peccauimus, we haue sinned good Lorde, we haue done
wickedlye , enter not into iudgement with vs, but be merciful vn
to vs after thy great mercye, and
accordynge to y multitude of thy
compassions, do away our iniqui
ties. &c. For in dede God is not
the god of Dauid only, Idem deus
Rom. r. omnium, he is the God of all: So
that Quicunque inuocauerit nomē
domini

domini ſalus erit, He oʒ ſhe whoſo
euer they be that call vppon the
name of ÿ loʒde, ſhalbe ſaued: In
confyʒmation whereof, this hiſto
rye is wʒitten, as are alſo the o-
ther, I haue recited, and manye
mo whiche I myghte recyte. As
of Manaſſes that wicked kinge,
whiche ſlewe Eſay the Pʒophet,
and wʒought verye muche wic-
kedneſſe, yet the Loʒde ſhewed
mercye vpon hym, beyng in pʒy-
ſon, as his pʒayer doth teach vs.
Nabugodonoʒar, thoughe foʒ a
time he bare gods anger, yet at ÿ
length he founde mercy. The ci-
tie of Niniue alſo founde fauour
with God, as dyd manye other,
which I wil omit foʒ tymes ſake
and wil bʒinge foʒth one oʒ twoo
out of the new teſtament, that we
maye ſe God, the ſeme God in ÿ
new teſtament he was in tholde.

Dan. iii

Iona. iii

G.ii.　　I might

I myght tell you of manye yf
I shoulde speake of ý Lunatike,
such as were possessed wt deupls,
lame, blinde, domme, deaf, lepers
&c. but tyme wyll not suffice me,
one or two therefore shall serue,
Mary Magdalene hadde seuen
deuylles, but yet they were caste
oute of hyr, and of all others, she
was the fyrst that Christe appea=
red vnto after his resurrection.

Joh.rr.

Thomas would not beleue chri=
stes resurrection thoughe manye
tolde hym whyche had seene and
felte hym, by reason whereof a
man myght haue thoughte, that
his synnes woulde haue cast him
awaye: excepte I shulde see & fele
(sayeth he) I wyll not beleue. Ah
wylfull Thomas: I wyll not
sayeth he, but Christe appeared
vnto hym, and woulde not leese
hym, as he will not do thee good
bro=

brother, yf that wyth Thomas
thou wylte kepe companye with
the disciples as Thomas dydde.
Peter his falle was vgglie, he ac
cursed hym selfe yf euer he knewe
Christe, and that for feare of a
gyrle, and this not once, but euen
three dyuers tymes, and that in
the hearynge of Christe his mai-
ster, but yet the thyrd time christe
loked backe, and cast on hym his
eye of grace, so that he wente out
and wept bitterly: and after christes resurrection not only dydde
the Aungels wyll the wemen to
tell Peter that Christe was rysen
but Christ hym self appeared vnto hym seuerallye: suche a good
Lorde is he.

The theefe hangynge on the
crosse, sayde but thus: Lord when
thou comest into thy kyngedome
remembre me, and what answere

Ioh. xx.

mat. xxvi
Lu. xxiiii

had

had her This daye sayth Christe

Lu. xxiii shalte thou be with me in paradyce. What a comfort is this, in
that he is nowe the same Christe,
to thee, and me, and vs all, yf we
wyll runne vnto him: For he is

Heb. xiii the same Christe to daye & to mo-
rowe, vntyll he come to iudge-
ment. Then in dede, he wylbe in
exorable, but nowe is he moore
ready to geue then thou to aske,
yf thou crye he heareth thee, yea
before thou crye. Crye therefore,

Esa. xxx. be bolde man, he is not parciall,
call sayth he, and I wyll heare
thee. Aske, and thou shalte haue,

Mat. vii. seke and thou shalte fynd, though
not at the fyrst, yet at the length,
yf he tarry a whyle, it is but to
trye thee. Nam veniens veniet, &
non tardabit. He is commyng and

Heb. x. wyl not be longe.

Thus haue you, iiii, meanes,
whick

which you must vſe to that ſay-
ning of fayth, oz certaine perſwa
ſiõ of gods mercy towardes you,
whiche is the ſecond part of pennaunce: namely, pzayer, the fre &
vniuerſall pzomiſes of Goodes
grace, the recozdation of the benefites of god paſt and pzeſente,
the exãples of gods mercy, whiche although they myght ſuffice,
yet wyll I put one moo to them,
whiche alonelye of it ſelfe is full
ſufficiente, I meane the deathe of
the ſonne of God Jeſus Chzſte,
which yf thou ſet befoze the eyes
of thy mynd it wyll confyzme thy
plackarde, foz it is the great ſeale
of Englande, as they ſaye, yea of
all the wozlde, foz the confyzma-
tion of all patentes and perpe-
tuities of the euerlaſtynge lyfe,
whervnto we are all called.

    Yf I thoughte theſe whyche
       I haue

I haue before recited, were not
sufficient to confyrme your fayth
of Gods loue towardes suche as
do repente, I woulde tarry longer herein: But because both I
haue bene longe, and also I trust
you haue some exercyse of conscience in this daylye (or els you
are to blame) I wyll but touche
and go. Consider with youre selues, what we are, misers, wret-
ches, and enemies to God: Consider what God is, euen he whiche hath al power, maieste, might
glorye, ryches, &c. perfectlye of
hymselfe, and neadeth nothynge,
but hath all thynges: Consider
what Christ is: Concernyng hys
godhead, coequall w his father,
euen he by whom all thynges were
made are ruled & gouerned: Concerninge his manhode, the onlye
Dearlyng of his father, in whome
is

is all his ioye . Nowe syz what a
loue is this,that this God , whi=
che neadeth nothynge,wold geue
wholly his owne selfe to thee his
ennemy,wzeaking hys wzath vp
on him selfe,in this his sonne, as
a man maye saye,to spare thee,to
saue thee,to wyn thee,to by thee,
to haue thee,toenioy the foz euer.

Because thy synne had sepe=
rated the from hym , to the ende
ÿ myghteste come eftsones into
hys company agayne,and therin
remayne,he hym selfe became as
a man wolde saye,a synner,oz ra=
ther synne it self, euen a maledic=
tion oz a curse : that we synners,
we accursed by his synne, that by
his oblation oz offeringe foz our
synnes,by his curse,might be de=
lyuered from synne,from maledic
tion . Foz by synne, he dstroyed
synne,killinge death,sathan,and
synne,

sinne, by theyr owne weapons, & that for thee & me (man) if we cast it not away by vnbeleif. Oh wonderful loue of god: who euer hard of such a loue: The father of heauen for vs his ennemies, to geue his owne deare son Jesus christ, and that not onely to be our brother, to dwell among vs, but also to the death of the crosse for vs: Oh wöderfull loue of christ to vs all: that was content & wyllinge to worke this feate for vs: Was there anye loue lyke to this loue:

God in dede hathe commended hys charitie and loue to vs herein, that when we were berye ennemyes vnto hym, he woulde geue his own sonne for vs: That we beyng men, might become as you would saye gods, God wold become mã: That we being mortall, might become immortal, the immor-

Rom. v.

immoztal God wold become moz
tal man: That we earthlye wzet-
ches mighte be sitizens of heaue,
the Lozde of heauen woulde become as a man wolde saye earthlye, that we beynge accursed,
myght be blessed, God wolde be
accursed: That we by our father
Adam beyng bzought oute of pa
radice, into the puddel of al pain,
myght be redemed, and bzoughte
into paradyce agayne, god wold
be our father, and an Adam ther
vnto: That we hauyng nothing,
might haue all thinges, God ha=
uynge all thynges, woulde haue
nothyng. That we beyng vessels
and slaues to all, euen to sathan ŷ
fend, myght be lozdes of all, and
of Sathan, the lozde of al would
become a vassal and a slaue to vs
all, and in daunger of Sathan:
Oh loue incompzehensible ⁊ who
                                    can

can otherwyse thynke nowe, but
yf the gratious good Lorde dis-
dayned not to geue hys owne
Sonne, his owne hartes ioye for
vs his verye ennemies, tofore we
thought to begge any such thing
at his hands, ye tofore we were:
who I say, can thinke otherwise,
but that with him he wil geue vs
all good thynges?

Yf when we hated hym, and
fledde awaye from hym, he sente
hys sonne to seke vs, who canne
thynke otherwyse, then y nowe we
louynge hym, and lamentynge
because we loue him no more, but
that he wyll for euer loue vs.
He that geueth the more to hys
ennemyes, wyll not he geue the
lesse trowe you to hys frendes?
God hath giuen his owne sonne,
then whyche thinge, nothynge is
greater to vs his ennemies, and
we

we nowe beyng become his fren=
des, wyll he denye vs fayth , and
pardone of oure synnes , whyche
thoughe they be greate, yet in
comparisone, nothynge at all.
Chꝛiste Jesus, woulde geue hys
owne selfe foꝛ vs , when we wyl=
led it not, and wil he nowe denye
vs fayth yf we wyll it.
This wyll is his earnest that he
hath geuen vs, truely to looke in Phil. ii.
dede,foꝛ the thynge wyled : And
loke thou foꝛ it in deede,foꝛ as he
hath geuen thee to wyll,so wyl he
geue thee to do.
   Jesus Chꝛist gaue his lyfe foꝛ
oure euylles , and by hys deathe
delyuered vs : Oh , then in that
he lyueth nowe , and cannet dye,
wyll he foꝛsake vs ? His hearte
bloude was not to derre foꝛ vs,
when we asked it not : what can
then be nowe to dere foꝛ vs , as=

kynge it is he a chaungelyng: is
he mutable as man is: can he repent hym of his gyftes ? Dyd he
not foresee our falles? payde not
he therefore the pryce. Because
he sawe we shulde fall sore, therfore wolde he suffer sore . Yea yf
his sufferynges hadde not bene
enoughe, he would yet once more
come agayne. G O D the father
I am sure, yf the death of hys
sonne incarnate wolde not serue,
woulde hym selfe and the holye
ghost also become incarnate, and
dye for vs. This death of Christ
therfore loke on, as ÿ very plege
of Gods loue towards the, whosoeuer thou arte, howe deepe soeuer thou hast sinned? See Gods
handes are nayled, they can not
stryke thee, his feete also, he cannot runne from thee, his armes
are wide open to imbrace the, his
heade

heade hanges down to kysse the,
his verye harte is open, so that
therin see, toote, looke, spie, pepe
and thou shalte se nothinge ther=
in but loue, loue, loue, loue, to the,
hide thee therefore, lay thy heade
there with the Euangeliste.
John.riii.

This is the clyfte of the rocke iii.re.rir
wherein Helias stode, this is the
pillow of downe, for al aking hea
des. Anoint thy head w this oile
let this oyntment enbaulme thy
heade, and washe the face: Tarry
thou here, and cock sure thou art
I warrent thee: Say w Paule, Ro. biii.
what can seperate me frō the loue
of god: can death, can pouertye,
sycknesse, hunger, or any myse=
ry perswade the nowe, that God
loueth the not: Say nothyng can
separate the frō the loue wher w
god hath loued p̄ in chrrist Iesus:

whome he loueth, he loueth to the
ende. John. xiii. So that nowe,
where aboundaunce of sinne hath
ben in thee, the moze is the aboundaunce of grace . But to what
ende ? forsooth that as sinne hath
raygned to death as thou seest,
to the kyllynge of Goddes sonne,
so now grace muste raigne to lyfe
to the honouryng of gods sonne,
who is nowe alyue, and cannot
dye any moze.

 So that they whiche by fayth
fele this cannot any moze dye to
GOD but to synne, wherto they
are dead and buried wyth christ.
As Christe therefore lyueth, so do
they, and that to God, to ryghtu-
ousnes and holynes . The lyfe
which they lyue is In fide filii dei,
in the fayth of the sonne of God,
whereby you see that now I am
slipt into that which I made the
     thyzde

thyrde parte of penaunce, namely newnes of lyfe, whych I could
not so haue done, yf that it were
a parte of it selfe in deede, as it is
an effect, a freewyt, of the seconde
parte that is of fayth or truste in
Gods mercy.

For he that beleueth, that is,
is certaynlye perswaded synne to
be such a thing that it is the cause
of al misery, and of it self so great
lye angreth God, that in heauen
nor in earth nothinge coulde appease his wrath saue alonely the
death & precíouse bloudshedinge
of the sonne of God, in whome is
all the delight and pleasure of the
father: He I say that is perswaded thus of sinne: the same cánot
but in hearte abhorre and quaue
to doe or saye, yea so thinke anye
thing willingly which Gods law
teachet hym to be sinne. Agayns

H.i.   he

he that beleueth, that is, is certaynlye perswaded Gods loue to
be so much towards him, ẙ wher
through synne he was loste, and
made a fyꝛe bꝛand of hel:the eternal Father of mercy,which is the
omnisufficient God,ᕋ nedeth nothing of vs,oꝛ of any thinge ẙ we
can do:to deliuer vs out of hell,ᕋ
to bꝛing vs into heauē, dyd sende
euē his own moste dere sonne out
of his bosome,out of heauen,into
hel as a man would say,to bꝛing
vs as I sayd frō thence, into his
owne bosome ᕋ mercy, we beyng
his very enemies:He I saye that
is thus perswaded of Gods loue
towardes him, ᕋ of ẙ pꝛice of his
redempcion, by the dere bloud of
the lābe imaculate Jesus Chꝛist:
the same mā cannot but loue god
again,ᕋ of loue do that,ᕋ hartley
desire to do better ẙ which might
please God. Trow you that such

a one knowig this geare by faith
wil willingly walter & wallow in
his woful luftes, plesure & lantis-
ftes. Wil suche a one as knoweth
bi faith chrift Jefus to haue geuē
his bloud, to wash him frō his fin
nes, play the fow to walter in his
puddell of fylthy finne & byre a-
gayn? Nay rather thē he wylbe
defiled agayn, by wilful finning,
he wil wash oftē the fete of his af
fecttiōs, watching ouer y vice ftil
fticking in him, which as a fpring
cōtinually fendeth out poyfon y-
nough to dzown & defile him, did
not the fwete water of Chriftes
paffion in gods fight wash it, and
his bloude fatiffic the rigoure of
Gods iuftice due foz the fame.
  This bloud of chrift fhed foz our
finnes, is to dere in the fighte of
him, that beleueth that he wil ab
hozre in his hart to ftampe it, and

treade it vnder his feete.

He knoweth nowe by his be-
lefe that it is to muche that he-
therto he hath set to little by it, &
is ashamed therof. Therfore the
respdue of hys lyfe he purposeth
to take better heede to him selfe
then to fore he dyd. For because
he seeth by his fayth the greuous
nes of Gods anger, the foulenes
of synne, the greatnesse of Gods
mercye, and of Christes loue towardes him, He wyll nowe be
headie, to praye God to geue him
his grace accordingly: that as w
his eyes, tonge, handes, feete. &c.
He hath displeased God doynge
his owne wyll, euen so now, with
the same eyes, tonge, eares, handes, feete. &c. He maye displease
his owne selfe, and do Gods wil.
Willinglye wyll he nowe do that
whiche mighte renewe the death
of

of the sonne of God: He knoweth
he hath to much sinne vnwilling
ly in hym, so that there to he wyll
not adde wylling offences.

This willing and witting of
sending, and sinning, whosoeuer
doeth flatter hym selfe therein,
doth euidentlye demonstrate and
shewe that he neuer yet in dede
taste of Christe truelye . He
was neuer truelye perswaded, or
beleued how foule a thynge synne
is how greuous a thinge Godes
anger is, howe ioyfull and preci-
ous a thing Gods mercy in christ
is, howe exceding broade , wyde,
highe and depe Christes loue is.
Perchaunce he can wryte, prate,
talke, and preache of this geare,
but yet he in hart by fayth, neuer
felte this geare . For dyd he once
feele this geare in dede, thē wolde
he be so farre from continuing in

synne willingly & wittingly, that
wholy & hartely, he wold geue o-
uer him self to ý which is cõtrari,
I meane to a new lyfe, renewing
his youth, euen as the Egle doth.
Psalm. ciii.

For as we being in ý seruitude
of sinne demonstrate our seruice
by geuyng ouer our mēbres to ý
obeyinge of synne frõ iniquitie to
iniquitie: euē so we beynge made
free from sinne by fayth in Iesus
Christ & endewed with gods spirite, a spirit of libertie. ii. Cor. iii.
must nedes demonstrate this fre-
dõ & libertie by geuinge ouer our
mēbres to thobediēce of ý spirite
by ý which we are led & gided frõ
vertue to vertue, & all kind of holynes. As thunbeleuers declare
their vnbeliefe by ý working of ý
euil spirit inthē. Eph. ii. outward
ly the fruites of the flesshe. Gal. v.

Euen

Euen so the beleuers declare
theyr fayth by the workinge of
gods good spyrit in the outwarde
ly the fruites of the sprite. For as
the deuyll is not deade in those
whiche are hys but worketh styll
to theyr dampnacion: so is not
God dead in them whiche be his
but worketh styll to their saluacion: the which working is not the
cause of ẏ one or thother being in
any, but only a demonstracion, a
signe, a fruit of thesame, as ẏ aple
is not the cause of ẏ aple tree, but
a fruite of it. Thus then you see
briefly that newnes of life is not
in dede a parte of penaunce but a
fruit of it, a demonstracion of the
iustifying fayth, a sygne of gods
good spirite possessing the hearte
of the penitent: As the old lyfe is
a frupte of impenitencie, a demõ-
straciõ of a lippe, faith or vnbelief

a signe of Sathans spirit possessing the heart of the impenitent, whiche al those be that be not penitent. For mean I knowe none, he that is not penitent, that same is impenitent, he that is not governed by Gods spirite, the same is governed by Sathans spirit. For all that be Christes are governed wyth the spirite of Christ, Rom. viii. which spirite hath her fruites, Gala. v. All other that be not Christes are the deuyls. He that gathereth not with Christe, scattereth abroade.

Therefore dearely beloued I beseche you to consyder this geare and deceaue not your selues. Yf you be not Christes, then pertain you to the deuyll, of which thinge the fruites of the fleshe doeth assure you, as whoredom, adultry, uncleanes, wantonnes, ydolatri, witch‐

witchcraft, enuie, strife, contenci-
on, wrathe, sedicion, murthers,
dronkenes, glottonie, blasphemy
slouthfulnes, ydlenes, baudy talking, sclaunderinge. &c. yf these
apples growe oute of the appele
trees of your harts, surely, surely the deuyl is at Inne with you
you are his byrdes, whom, when
he hath wel fed you, he wyl broch
you and eate you, chaw you, and
champ you, world without ende
in eternall wo and miserie. But
I am otherwyse perswaded of
you al: I trust you be al Christes
Iesus his people and childre, yea
brethren by fayth.

As ye see your sinnes in Gods
lawe and tremble syghe, sorow, &
sob for the same, euen so you see
his great mercies in his Gospell
and free promises, and therefore
are glad, merrie, and ioyefull for
that

that you are accepted into Gods
fauour, haue your sinnes pardoned, & are endued w̃ þ good spirit
of God, euẽ the seale & signe ma-
nuell of your electiõ in Christ before the beginning of the worlde.

The which spirite, for that he
is the spirit of life geuẽ to you, to
worke in you, with you, & by you
here in this lyfe, sanctificatiõ and
holynes where vnto you are called, that ye might be holy euen as
your heauenlye father is holye: I
beseche you all by admoniciõ &
warnynge of you that you wolde
stirre vp the giftes of God geuen
to you generally & particulerli to
þ edifying of hys Church, that is
I praye you that you woulo not
moleste the good spyryte of God
by rebellinge agaynste it, when it
prouoketh and calleth you to go
on forewardes, that he whyche is
holy

II. Cor. i.

1. Thes.
iiii.

1. Petr. i.

II. Tim. i

Eph. iiii

holy, myght yet be moꝛe holy, he Ap. rril.
whiche is righteous myghte be
moꝛe righteous. As the euyll ſpi-
reſe moutth and ſtirreth vp the
ſylthy, to be yet moꝛe ſyllthy, the
couetous, to be moꝛe couetous,
the wicked to be moꝛe wicked.

Declare you now your repentaunce by woꝛkes of repentaūce
bꝛing foꝛth fruites, and woꝛthye
fruytes, lette youre ſoꝛowing foꝛ
your euyls demonſtrate it ſelfe,
by departinge frō the euyls you
haue vſed, let your certayntie of
pardon of your ſinnes thꝛoughe
Chꝛiſte and youre ioye in hym be
demonſtrated by purſuing of the
good thinges which gods woꝛde
teacheth you: you are nowe in
Chꝛiſt Ieſus gods woꝛkmāſhip Ephe. ii.
to doo good woꝛkes, whiche God
hath pꝛepared foꝛ you to walk in   Titus. ii
foꝛ the grace of God ꝥ bꝛyngeth
                     ſaluacion

saluacion vnto al men hath apea
red, & teachzth vs that we should
denie vngodlines, and worldlye
lustes, and that we should liue so
brelye, ryghteouslye and godly in
this present worlde, lokynge for
that blessed hope, and glorious
apearing of the mighty God, and
of oure Sauiour Jesus Christe,
which gaue him self for vs, to re=
deme vs from al vnrighteousnes
and to purge vs a peculier people
vnto him self, feruently geuē vn=
to good werkes. Titus.ii.

Agayne Titus.iii. for we our
selues also were in times past vn
wyse, disobediente, deceaued, in
daunger to lustes, and to dyuers
maners of voluptuousnes, liuing
in malic]ousnes and enuie, full of
hate, hating one another. But af=
ter that the kyndnes and loue of
God our Sauiour, to manward
appearl

appeared, not by ý dedes of righteousnes which we wrought, but of his mercye he saued vs, by the fountayne of the newe byrth, and with the renuing of the holy gost which he shed on vs aboundantly thorow Iesus Christ our Sautoure, that we once iustifyed by his grace, should be heires of eternal lyfe through hope. This is a true saying: but I wyll make an ende for I am to tedious.

Dearely beloued repent your synnes, that is be sorye, for that which is past, beleue in gods mercy for pardon, how depely soeuer you haue synned, & both purpose and earnestly pursue a newe lyfe, bringinge forth worthy and true fruytes of repentaunce.

As you haue geuen ouer your members, from synne to sinne, to serue the deuyl: your tongues to
sweare

sweare, to lye, to flatter, to skolde,
to iest, to skoffe, to baudy talke, to
vayne iangeling, to boasting. &c.
Your hādes to picking, groping,
idlenes, fightyng. &c. your fete to
skippig, goyng to euil, to dausing
&c. youre eares to heare fables,
lyes, vanities, & euil thinges. &c.
So now geue ouer your mēbres
to godlines, your tonge to speake
youre eares to heare, youre eyes
to see, your mouthes to tast, your
haudes to woorke , youre feete
to go about such thinges, as may
make to Gods glorie, sobrietie of
lyfe, & loue to your brethē, & that
dayly more & more diligently: for
in a stay to stand you cānot, ether
better or woorse you are to daye
then you were yesterdaye.

But better I trust you be & wil
be yf you marke wel my theme, þ
is repēt you, þ which thing þ you
wold

wold do, as before I haue humblye
be sought you: euē so now yet once
more I do agayn besech you, & ye
for the tender mercies of God in
Christ Iesus our lord, Repēt you
repēt you, for ye kingdō of heauē
that is, a kingdomful of al riches
pleasures, myrth, beautie, swete
nes, & eternal felicitie is at hand.
The eye hath not sene the lyke, ye
eare hath not hearde the like, the
hearte of mā cannot conceaue the
treasures & plesures of this king
dō, which now is at hand, to such
as repent, ye is to such as are sory
for their sinnes, beleue gods mer
cy through christ, & earnestly pur
pose to lead a new life: the god of
mercye through Christ his sonne
graūt vs his holy spiret & worke
in our hearts this sorow, fayth, &
new life which through his grace
I haue spoken of, both now & for
euer. A M E N.

i. Cor. ii.
esa. lxiiii